RONALD J. DREZ

remember d-day

The Plan, the Invasion, Survivor Stories

 NATIONAL GEOGRAPHIC

Washington, D.C.

To my wife, children, and grandchildren
for their love and inspiration.

John M. Fahey, Jr., *President and Chief Executive Officer*
Gilbert M. Grosvenor, *Chairman of the Board*
Nina D. Hoffman, *Executive Vice President,*
  President of Books and Education Publishing Group
Ericka Markman, *Senior Vice President, President of Children's*
  Books and Education Publishing Group

STAFF FOR THIS BOOK
Nancy Laties Feresten, *Vice President, Editor-in-Chief of*
  Children's Books
Suzanne Patrick Fonda, *Project Editor*
Bea Jackson, *Art Director, Children's Books*
Janet Dustin, *Illustrations Coordinator*
David M. Seager, *Designer*
Carl Mehler, *Director of Maps*
NGMaps and Gregory Ugiansky, *Map Research*
  and Production
Connie D. Binder, *Indexer*
Judith Klein, *Copy Editor*
R. Gary Colbert, *Production Director*
Lewis R. Bassford, *Production Manager*
Vincent P. Ryan, *Manufacturing Manager*

Text is set in ITC New Baskerville.

One of the world's largest nonprofit scientific and educational
organizations, the National Geographic Society was founded in 1888
"for the increase and diffusion of geographic knowledge." Fulfilling this
mission, the Society educates and inspires millions every day through
its magazines, books, television programs, videos, maps and atlases,
research grants, the National Geographic Bee, teacher workshops, and
innovative classroom materials. The Society is supported through
membership dues, charitable gifts, and income from the sale of its
educational products. This support is vital to National Geographic's
mission to increase global understanding and promote conservation of
our planet through exploration, research, and education. For more
information, please call 1-800-NGS LINE (647-5463) or write to the
following address:

NATIONAL GEOGRAPHIC SOCIETY
1145 17th Street N.W.
Washington, D.C. 20036-4688 U.S.A.

Visit the Society's Web site: www.nationalgeographic.com

Printed in Belgium

ACKNOWLEDGMENTS
Special thanks to Dr. Douglas Brinkley, Kevin Willey, and Michael
Edwards of the Eisenhower Center and the staff of the National
D-Day Museum in New Orleans. They continue the work of the late
Dr. Stephen E. Ambrose, my friend and mentor. Thanks also to my
editor, Suzanne Patrick Fonda, who worked to make this story so
very special. Finally, to the men of D-Day to whom we all owe a
measure of our freedom.

Drez, Ronald J., 1940-
Remember D-day : the plan, the invasion, survivor stories / written
by Ronald J. Drez.—1st ed.; foreword by David Eisenhower
    p. cm.
Summary: Discusses the events and personalities involved in the
momentous Allied invasion of France on June 6, 1944.
  ISBN 0-7922-6666-8 (trade edition)
  ISBN 0-7922-6965-9 (library edition)
1. World War, 1939-1945—Campaigns—France—Normandy—
Juvenile literature. 2. Operation Overlord—Juvenile literature. 3.
World War, 1939–1945—Germany—Juvenile literature. [1. World
War, 1939–1945—Campaigns—France—Normandy. 2. Operation
Overlord.] I. Title.
  D756.5.N6D74 2004
  940.54'21421—dc22

                                        2003017733

PHOTO CREDITS
Cover, Franklin D. Roosevelt Library; 4–5, National Archives; 7
(upper, center), National Archives; 8, Bettmann/CORBIS; 10, Hulton
Archive/Getty Images; 11, National D-Day Museum; 12, Imperial
War Museum; 13 (upper), Imperial War Museum; 13 (lower),
Imperial War Museum; 14, Franklin D. Roosevelt Library; 15,
National D-Day Museum; 16, Alexandra Boulat; 17, National
Archives; 18 (left), Bettmann/CORBIS; 18 (right), UPI/Bettmann/
CORBIS; 20, Alexandra Boulat; 21, Art Museum, Naval Historical
Foundation; 22, Bettmann/CORBIS; 23, Mark Thiessen/Collection of
Joe Vaghi; 24, recreated with the permission of the *London Daily
Telegraph;* 25, AP/Wide World Photos; 26, Public Record Office,
United Kingdom; 27 (both), Bletchley Park, www.bletchleypark.org.uk;
28, National Archives; 29, National D-Day Museum; 30–31, Imperial
War Museum; 32 (upper), Official U.S. Army Air Forces; 32 (lower),
Imperial War Museum; 33, National D-Day Museum; 34 (right),
National D-Day Museum; 34 (left), Imperial War Mueum; 36, U.S.
Signal Corps; 37, Bettmann/CORBIS; 39, Hulton-Deutsch
Collection/CORBIS; 40, CORBIS; 41 (upper), National D-Day
Museum; 41 (lower), U.S. Army; 42 (left), National D-Day Museum;
42 (right), Michael St. Maur Sheil/CORBIS; 43 (upper), National D-Day
Museum; 43 (lower), National D-Day Museum; 44, Art Museum,
Naval Historical Foundation; 45, National D-Day Museum; 48
(upper), Owen Franken/CORBIS; 48 (lower), National D-Day
Museum; 49, Imperial War Museum; 50 (upper), National Archives;
50 (lower), Robert Capa/MAGNUM; 51, National D-Day Museum; 52,
National D-Day Museum; 53 (upper), National Archives; 53 (lower),
National Archives; 54, National D-Day Museum; 55, Official U.S.
Navy Photograph from Acme; 56, National D-Day Museum; 59, Art
Museum, Naval Historical Foundation; 60, National D-Day Museum.

COVER: American soldiers make their way to shore at Normandy
on D-Day, June 6, 1944.

TITLE PAGE: The first wave of troops faces heavy fire from German
guns at Omaha Beach.

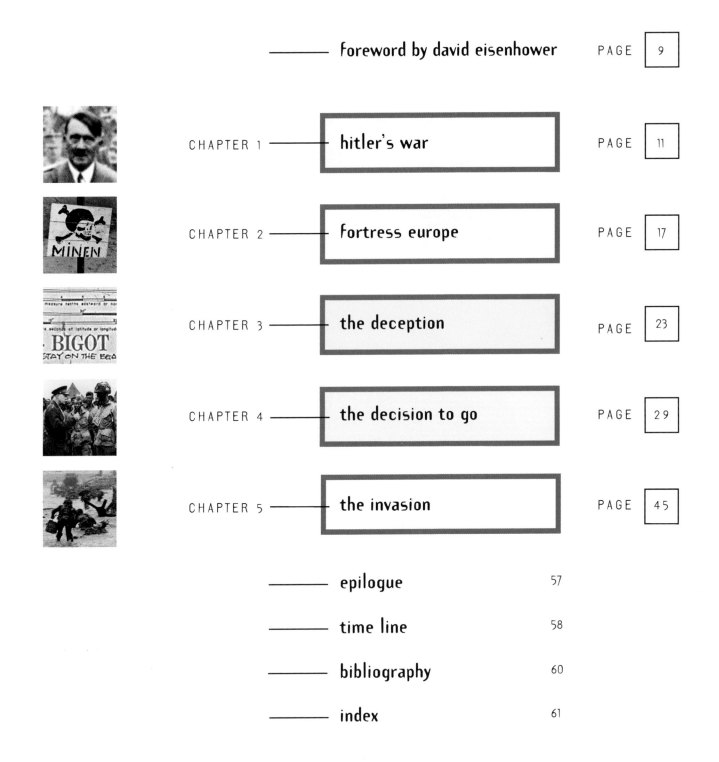

General Dwight David Eisenhower, Supreme Commander of Allied forces on D-Day, meets his grandson and namesake (right) for the first time during a brief trip home from Europe in 1951. With them are grandmother Mamie and sister Anne.

Foreword

My grandfather never spoke to me much about the war. He seemed reluctant to talk about any aspect of it. Yet he did not discourage me as a boy from watching and re-watching a TV documentary based on his memoir *Crusade in Europe*. He knew that the war was the defining period of his life, as it was for everyone who lived through it, and he knew that future generations would look back carefully on a time when the lives and hopes of not just millions of people but of civilization itself hung precariously in the balance. He also was very aware that his decisions as Supreme Commander always entailed serious costs and sacrifice.

D-Day, June 6, 1944, was the decisive moment of the decisive campaign to gain victory in Europe in World War II. It opened the vital second front against Germany, spelling ultimate defeat for the Nazis. But in hindsight, the intangible significance of D-Day is even greater. It meant that, after decades of doubt and hesitation, democracy, freedom, and the humane values championed by the Western Allies resumed the offensive. It marked the beginning of a long march to victory that finally ended with the unification of Europe in 1990, the centennial of Granddad's birth.

In 1982, my wife and I visited the places described in this book. We hiked along the Normandy beaches, strolled through the towns, and visited the cemeteries. In southern England, which had been one huge military encampment in late May and early June 1944, we saw where Granddad had dropped in on the 101st Airborne Division to wish the troops "Godspeed." In my mind's eye I could easily see the caravans of vehicles streaming toward the docks, passing through quaint towns where villagers came out to wave good-bye and wish good luck to the soldiers. I remembered the words Granddad wrote to the soldiers, sailors, and airmen in his D-Day proclamation, "The eyes of the world are upon you. The hopes and prayers of liberty-loving people everywhere march with you."

These sites live on as monuments to the ingenuity, bravery, and the highest ideals of citizenship that the soldiers of D-Day exemplified. At the outset of World War I President Wilson proclaimed, "Right is more precious than peace." The soldiers of D-Day were called upon to bear witness to that belief.

Amid the accounts that offer personal glimpses into the private thoughts of people involved in D-Day is one about British admiral Sir Bertram Ramsay. One week before the attack, Ramsay said, "It is a tragic situation that this is a scene of a stage set for terrible human sacrifice, but if out of it comes peace and happiness, who would have it otherwise?"

At a heavy price in lives, D-Day did bring victory, and in the goodness of time, peace and happiness did come. Why and how it happened will be remembered as long as people remember our day and time. Would anyone today have it otherwise?

David Eisenhower

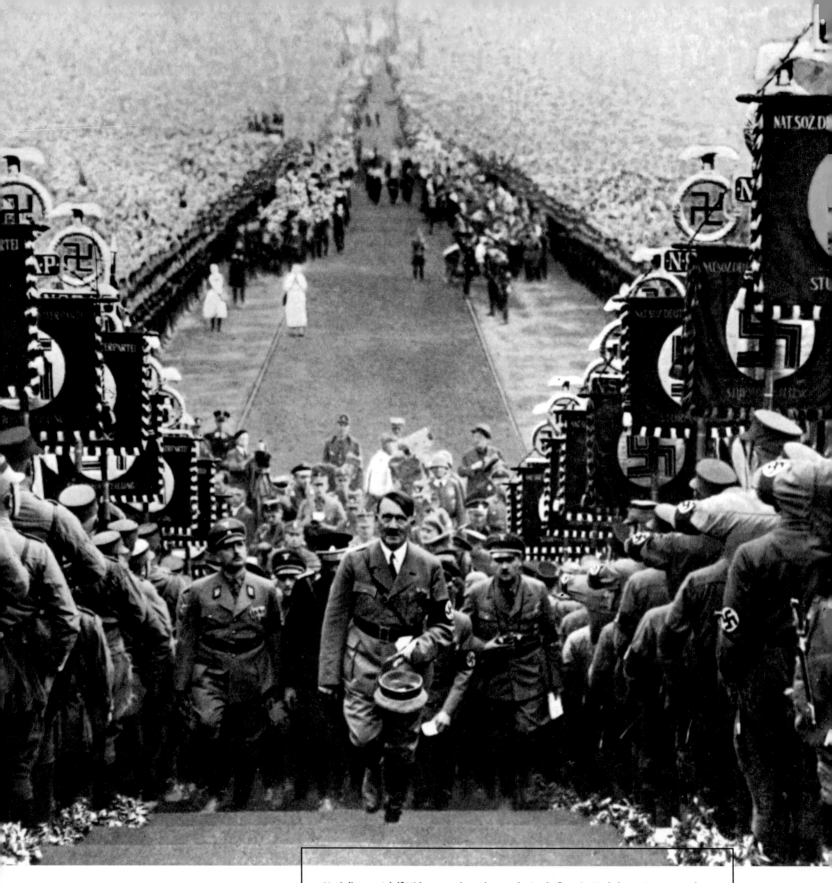

Nazi dictator Adolf Hitler ascends to the speaker's platform in Bückeburg, Germany, where he will address a massive party rally in 1934. His meteoric rise to enormous power was the result of his success in guiding Germany out of both economic and political depression.

CHAPTER 1

hitler's war

In 1938 the German Army began to occupy territory and countries in Western Europe. First they reclaimed the Rhineland, land west of the Rhine River that Germany had lost as a result of its defeat in World War I. When Great Britain and France did not challenge the act, German dictator Adolf Hitler used military force to take over Austria and much of Czechoslovakia (now two countries, the Czech Republic and Slovakia). Still Britain and France did nothing. But when Hitler massed his armies on the border of Poland, Britain and France announced that an invasion there would lead them to declare war against Germany. Hitler ignored the warning. On September 1, 1939, his armies invaded Poland. The speed with which they conquered that country shocked the world.

The armies of Britain and France dug in along the French border facing Germany and awaited a massive onslaught. For six months, the opposing armies faced each other across that border in what became known as the "phony war." Finally, on May 10, 1940, Germany launched a massive invasion through Belgium, splitting the British and French Armies. Most of the British Army (but not its equipment) was saved through a dramatic seaborne rescue from the French beaches at Dunkirk. The French Army surrendered, and, like Poland, France was overrun in a month. By the summer of 1940 most people in Western Europe had lost their freedom and were living under Nazi control (see map page 19). Jews in particular were denied all their rights, even the right to live.

A swastika, insignia of Hitler's Nazi Party, decorates an armband and a German Army helmet.

Hitler now turned his attention to England. The British people armed themselves and blacked out their lights at night so the Luftwaffe, as the German Air Force was called, could not easily target them. Buildings were camouflaged, and barbed wire went up everywhere, even around London's most famous landmark: the clock tower and bell known as Big Ben. Children were moved out of the cities to the countryside, where they would be safer.

On July 10, 1940, the air war known as the Battle of Britain began with a mighty

During the bombing of London, which began in September 1940, children were sent to the countryside for safety. The bombing was called the Blitz (short for the German word *blitzkrieg,* meaning "lightning war") because of the speed with which the attacks were made.

bombing campaign over southern England that continued for three months. More than 15,000 tons of bombs fell on Britain during that time, but the Germans could not sweep the Royal Air Force from the sky or break the spirit of the British people.

Having failed to conquer Britain, Hitler turned his attention eastward. In June 1941 his armies invaded the Soviet Union. Six months later on December 7, 1941, the Japanese attacked the U.S. military base at Pearl Harbor, Hawaii. The next day the United States declared war on Japan. Three days later Germany declared war on the United States.

America mobilized. Young men joined the armed forces to fight. Many young women also joined the Army and Navy in supporting roles. Suddenly plants and factories making trucks, planes, tanks, and ships found women filling jobs vacated by men called to war. Schoolchildren learned about rationing and recycling to save materials needed to fight the war, and high schoolers were offered courses in the safe use of weapons. Families planted "victory gardens" in support of the war effort.

In 1942 the United States began shipping armed forces along with thousands of tons of weapons, supplies, and munitions to England as part of the buildup for an eventual attack on Nazi-controlled Europe. Soviet leader Joseph Stalin, whose armies were still fighting the Germans in the east, was demanding that the British and Americans open a new battle front by attacking Europe from the west. He said that if

This poster captures the determination of people in Britain to survive the German air raids, which continued until March 1945. The scene of St. Paul's Cathedral, rising above the smoke and flames of a night bombing raid over London (below), became a symbol of the endurance of the British people.

the Allies failed to do this, he could not guarantee that his blood-drained country could continue to fight. Britain and America knew that without the Soviets in the war, Germany could concentrate all of its military might against an invasion from the west. So they promised to invade the continent from across the English Channel.

On December 7, 1943, exactly two years after the Japanese attack on Pearl Harbor, President Franklin Roosevelt scribbled a note to Stalin in which he named General Dwight David Eisenhower as commander of Operation Overlord, code name for the Allied invasion of Europe. As Supreme Commander of the Allied forces, Eisenhower would try to become the first man in the history of the world to invade the mainland of Europe from Britain.

Finally, in 1944, the Allies were strong enough to stage the invasion. For five long years the people of Europe had been at war, and they had died by the millions. The world prayed and yearned for freedom and an end to Nazi terror. If successful, an invasion across the English Channel would bring about the beginning of the end of the Nazi nightmare. If the attack failed, Hitler would continue his murderous rule.

In the United States people of all ages helped in the war effort. Here, two grand-mothers work in a munitions factory loading bullets into clips for rifles that will be shipped overseas.

THE GUY WHO RELAXES IS HELPING THE AXIS!

At the Higgins Boat Works in New Orleans, Louisiana, the landing craft that will be used in the amphibious assault on the beaches of Normandy on D-Day are assembled. The sign overhead reminds workers that laziness helps the enemy.

The menacing gun at the German battery at Longues-sur-Mer aims out into the English Channel. Now silent, it stands as a monument to D-Day.

fortress europe

Where would the British and American forces attack? This was the big question for the Allies and Hitler alike. In January 1944 the Atlantic Wall of Hitler's *Festung Europa* (Fortress Europe) extended for 3,500 miles from Norway down to Denmark and across the Netherlands, Belgium, and France to the Bay of Biscay. It was not a wall made of bricks and stone, but it was called that because it was fortified with concrete defenses manned by the German Army. The most obvious place for the invasion was Calais in northern France, just 25 miles across the Channel from the British port of Dover. Hitler recognized this as the most likely site and greatly strengthened German defenses around this area. But since he could not predict for certain where an Allied invasion would strike, he could not afford to concentrate his soldiers in one spot. He had to spread them out.

To command the German forces defending the Atlantic Wall, Hitler chose Field Marshal Erwin Rommel. Hitler told him of the importance of the upcoming battle. "When the enemy invades in the west," he said, "it will be the moment of decision in this war." Hitler knew that victory would be his if he could defeat the invasion.

Rommel inspected the defenses along the English Channel and was disappointed at the lack of prepared positions and fortifications. Except at Calais, Dieppe, and Cherbourg, the rest of the defenses were weak. He immediately ordered the laying of millions of mines along the beaches and in the water and had his engineers begin building coastal fortifications made of concrete and steel that housed huge guns.

He knew that these measures would only slow down an invasion. To defeat the invasion he needed to meet the attackers on the beaches and crush them with superior armor. To accomplish this he requested that the German tanks (Panzers) be moved closer to the coast. Here he ran into a problem. His immediate superior, Field Marshal Gerd von Rundstedt, said no.

On the other side of the English Channel, General Eisenhower was facing his own problems. The first of these was deciding where in France to land. The landing

German sign warns of a minefield. Some marked real danger; others were decoys to fool the enemy.

German Field Marshal Erwin Rommel (above) was in charge of defenses at Normandy. At right, German soldiers charged with putting obstacles on Omaha Beach at low tide run as an Allied reconnaissance plane flies over.

beaches had to be within the range of air support flying from England. The Army also had to be resupplied once it landed. This meant there had to be an area where unloading operations could take place. Eisenhower didn't even consider attacking the French ports directly. They were too well defended to attack from the sea. Eisenhower reasoned that a port would have to be attacked from the rear and then captured after a successful landing on the beaches.

Europe: June 6, 1944

This map shows how much of Europe had fallen under Nazi control by June 1944. Germany's boundaries include the lands that had become part of the country after Hitler annexed them in 1938: the Rhineland, Austria, and the part of Czechoslovakia known as Sudetenland. The remaining part of that country was Slovakia.

Eisenhower realized that the Germans would expect the invasion fleet to cross the English Channel at its narrowest point—between Dover and Calais. So he and his planners chose to land in the area that was the longest distance across the Channel: the beaches of Normandy. He was willing to undertake the hundred-mile distance if it meant that he could surprise the enemy.

Why Normandy? First of all, enemy fortifications there were not too strong, and the area was away from the great German reserve forces. But most important, the Normandy area offered a number of suitable beaches on which to land.

Eisenhower's next problem was to make sure that the German Army could not react quickly to the attack once it realized what he was up to. To ensure this, he ordered planes to bomb bridges, railroads, and roadways so the German Army couldn't move reinforcements to the battlefield. But for every bomb dropped in the Normandy area, two were dropped elsewhere so the Germans wouldn't know that the Allies were interested in Normandy. The air offensive against German transportation was devastating. More than 900 locomotives and 16,000 freight cars were destroyed.

Another problem facing the Allies was that Normandy had no deepwater ports. Without such ports, Eisenhower would be unable to get fresh supplies to his army. Even if the invasion were initially successful, it would eventually fail.

The sheltered cove at the French town of Arromanches-les-Bains was selected by the Allies as the site of one of the artificial harbors code-named Mulberry. The other was farther west at Omaha Beach.

The Germans were aware of the problems Normandy posed to the Allies. The lack of port facilities led them to conclude that Normandy was not a real threat as an invasion site. What the Germans didn't know was that the Allies had figured out a way to solve their port problem. They began planning and building an artificial port that could be towed across the Channel by giant sea tugs to Normandy after the beaches had been secured. There, it would be assembled to substitute for the lack of an existing port. They called this remarkable project Mulberry.

Never before had an army tried to take its harbors with it. Engineers and construction experts were gathered from all over England. They were told to figure out a way to build two harbors, each the size of Britain's port of Dover, in 150 days. The idea the engineers came up with was to sink old ships and huge concrete breakwaters called Phoenix caissons in an arch around the seaside town of Arromanches-les-Bains and off the Normandy beach code-named Omaha. These structures would break up the action of the waves in the English Channel, creating calm water between the caissons and the beach. Then roads and piers would be run on pontoons from the caissons to the beach (see page 55).

The Phoenixes were enormous. Each was almost 70 feet long and weighed more than 6,000 tons. There was enough material in just one of them to construct 50 miles of interstate highway. To make the two artificial harbors, 147 of these giant structures were needed. One reporter later described one of them as looking like "Noah's Ark without a roof."

All over southern England more than 30,000 workers began constructing the parts of the two Mulberry Harbors. Work on this top-secret project went at a feverish pace during the early months of 1944, as the engineers tried to meet the impossible schedule for readiness. As D-Day (the name for the actual day of the invasion) approached, the workers had achieved the impossible. Now, all that remained was for Operation Neptune, the cross-Channel amphibious invasion, to be successful.

A Phoenix caisson takes shape at a dockyard in England. More than 70 of these 6,000-ton structures were needed to make each of the two Mulberry Harbors, which would be towed across the Channel and sunk to create a breakwater along the Normandy coast.

By scattering rubber tanks (like the one shown here) and trucks around the British countryside, the Allies made the Germans think they had more troops and equipment than they really had. Many were placed around Dover to convince the German High Command that the attack would come at Calais, far from Normandy.

the deception

Eisenhower knew that Operation Neptune would fail if the Germans learned the location of the landing site. So it was important for the Allies to deceive the Germans as to where and when they would attack, while at the same time keeping their real plans a secret. As the days of 1944 drew closer to D-Day, secrecy became an obsession. Any leak of the plan could mean disaster for the invasion and the men making the landing.

General Eisenhower gave strict orders that anyone who broke the rules of secrecy would be subject to harsh discipline. The press was censored, and telegrams and mail were monitored to ensure that the Neptune secret was not leaked. Even travel in England was restricted. Operation Neptune had a special security classification called BIGOT that was higher than Top Secret. Only people with the BIGOT clearance could see information about the Neptune plan.

But as with any operation of such huge size, there were leaks. On one occasion, an American officer who was a friend of General Eisenhower's casually mentioned at a party that the invasion would be launched before June 15. When Eisenhower heard of this, he reduced the officer three ranks from major general to lieutenant colonel and sent him home.

Other incidents happened that made the Allies think that the Germans had discovered the plan. During an air raid over London, enemy bombs fell on the street where an intelligence officer was carrying the plan in a briefcase. The man was killed instantly, and the briefcase, with the plan, was never found. The Allies could only hope that it had been burned in the explosion, but they were not certain that it had not fallen into enemy hands.

Then a curious series of crossword puzzles appeared in a British daily newspaper. In five puzzles appearing just before D-Day, key code words of the invasion plan appeared as answers. Those words were: Omaha, Utah, Mulberry, Overlord, and Neptune. These were the names of the two American invasion beaches, the artificial harbor project, the overall Allied invasion strategy, and most important, the cross-

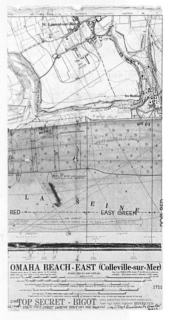

Map of the operational plan for Omaha Beach is stamped "Top Secret—BIGOT," meaning it could be seen only by people with the highest security clearance.

The code name "Mulberry" appeared as the answer to 11 Across in a crossword puzzle published in a British newspaper a week before D-Day. The clue was "This bush is centre of nursery revolutions."

Channel attack plan. The probability of coincidence was astronomically low. The two professors who made up the puzzles were questioned, but investigators could not prove any sinister connection. The case was closed.

Secrecy alone would not be enough to safeguard Operation Neptune. If the invasion were to have a chance to succeed, the Allies would have to fool the Germans about where and when the attack would take place. The British were especially good at intelligence and deception. They had learned in previous wars that nothing substituted for good intelligence. In 1943, after enduring four years of war, British Prime Minister Winston Churchill told President Franklin Roosevelt that "in wartime truth is so precious she should always be attended by a bodyguard of lies." He was speaking of a scheme to deceive the German High Command into thinking the attack was coming at someplace other than Normandy. So as the war progressed, so did a secret war of plots and counterplots, tangles within tangles, double agents, false agents, and treachery. Deceptions and lies were intermingled with tantalizing bits of truth in tales to deceive Adolf Hitler.

The German spy agency was called *Abwehr,* and it attempted to counter the Allied intelligence machine. It dropped its own agents by parachute into England and landed other agents by rubber boats from ships and submarines. Soon, radios in Germany crackled with news from these agents, who sent secret messages from inside England about troop concentrations, hidden airfields, and other information about the buildup for the invasion. The Germans were pleased with their steady stream of spy message traffic. They felt that they were keeping informed on the details of the Allied planning.

But what the Germans didn't know was that their spy mission was a total disaster. Incredibly, every spy that they had placed in England had been captured. The British made those captured spies an offer that was hard to refuse. They could become double agents and work for England while appearing to work for Germany, or they could face the hangman's noose. Most chose to become double agents. Without knowing it, the Abwehr had fallen victim to a gigantic deception operation called Operation Doublecross.

Doublecross fooled the Germans, but it became a potential disaster for the British and the Americans. The information fed to the Germans through the spy message traffic

Winston Churchill, shown here with General Dwight D. Eisenhower, Supreme Commander of Operation Overlord, recognized the key role deception would play in determining the success or failure of the Allied mission.

This photograph of Allied double agent Garbo is from British Intelligence files. His real name, Juan Pujol, was not revealed until long after the war.

had to be true but harmless to the Allied plans. It had to lead the enemy to draw the desired conclusions. In this dangerous game, one discovered lie, one blatant falsehood, could collapse Operation Doublecross like a house of cards. And if Doublecross collapsed, all the double agents would be exposed and most likely killed, and the real invasion plan would be revealed.

It is hard to imagine the difficulty of this operation. Agents had to tell lies and then continue the deception with other lies, always having to remember the ones they told so the enemy wouldn't discover the double cross.

One particularly successful agent had the code name Garbo. He had the unique ability of keeping his 20 different identities separate and never confusing his stories. Acting as an independent agent, he convinced the Germans that he was loyal to them when in fact he was loyal to the British. Because the Germans trusted him, Garbo was able to create fictitious Allied armies in the minds of the Germans. Through false message traffic and deception, the Allies were able to convince Hitler that General Eisenhower had 89 divisions ready for D-Day when he only had 47.

In addition to the deception by Garbo and other agents, several dozen middle-aged British officers in remote areas of England and Scotland produced a military illusion. By sending out messages ordering skis and cold weather clothing and snowshoes, these few officers and some radio operators created in the German mind a fictitious British Fourth Army, with a strength of 250,000 men capable of invading Norway.

The United States also concocted an army under General George S. Patton that was not completely fictitious but that was only a fraction of its reported strength. The Germans considered Patton to be the Allies' best general. So General Eisenhower took advantage of this and stationed General Patton at Dover, the British port directly across the Channel from Calais. Engineers and technicians constructed rubber tanks and trucks and parked them all over the countryside so they would be photographed by German planes.

Camps were constructed and tents set up to look as though they were occupied by American troops. Loudspeakers played the recorded sounds of vehicles and tanks and camp activity so that it could be heard in the surrounding towns. Guards were posted at the entrances, and vehicles moved in and out, but few soldiers were inside.

The Germans thought messages sent by their Enigma encoder (below) could not be "broken." But Royal Navy personnel (left) used a huge computer at a top-secret facility named Bletchley Park to do just that. As a result, they were able to listen to German message traffic throughout the war.

As a result of these deceptions, Hitler reinforced his forces in Norway and placed his best army around Calais, far from Normandy. But the Allies had more up their sleeves.

As the day of invasion drew close, a final, dangerous plot was planned. On the day that General Eisenhower launched the invasion, Garbo would reveal the plan to the Germans! But it would be told in such a fashion that as it passed through the German command and worked its way down each level until it reached the forces guarding the beaches, it would be too late to be of any use. By that time the Allied soldiers would be storming ashore.

But to the Germans, this incredible information would raise Garbo's reputation to a new high, and that is just what the Allies wanted. When the German Army began to react to the invasion, then Garbo would spring the trap. He would tell the Germans that the invasion coming ashore at Normandy was a hoax. It was just a diversion meant to fool the German Army. The real invasion, under General Patton, was ready to strike Calais from Dover as soon as the German forces at Calais began moving toward Normandy.

Because of Garbo's credibility with German intelligence, the Allies hoped the Germans would believe him and hold their massive armies in place so the Normandy invasion would have a chance to get ashore successfully.

In preparation for the invasion, equipment is loaded into the cavernous cargo holds of LSTs (Landing Ship Tanks) docked in southern England. Once across the Channel, the ships will run right up on the beach and unload men, vehicles, and weapons.

the decision to go

The first few days of June were perfect for invasion: clear skies, little wind, and warm sunshine. The Allied commanders were delighted that good weather might prevail for D-Day, scheduled for Monday, June 5. Everything was loaded, and ships began to sail out of their harbors to form up in convoys heading to Normandy. More than 3,000 ships would make up 75 convoys and follow the minesweepers toward the French coast. But on June 3, the weather began to change. The forecast was for rain with low clouds from Sunday through Wednesday, and a four-foot surf on the beaches along the French coast.

At 4 a.m. on June 4 at Southwick House, Allied headquarters in Portsmouth, England, General Eisenhower held a final conference on the weather. Group Captain J.M. Staggs, head of the weather office, had a frown on his face. Although skies were clear and the stars shining, he announced that on June 5 there would be hurricane-force winds. Worse still, his ability to make accurate predictions during this period was limited.

For General Eisenhower, this was bad news. "The mighty force was tense as a coiled spring," the general said. The men, vehicles, and equipment were on board ship. How long could they stay there before the enemy discovered that the invasion was poised to begin? Ike asked his subordinates to give him their opinions. General Montgomery wanted to go; the other British generals, Sir Arthur Tedder and Sir Trafford Leigh-Mallory, wanted to postpone. British Admiral Sir Bertram Ramsay said that the Navy could do its job, but the Higgins Boats that would carry the soldiers to the beaches would be hard to control.

Eisenhower listened to all and then made his decision. At 6 a.m. he ordered a delay of one day. They would try to go on June 6. He announced that they would meet again at 9:30 that night to restudy the weather forecast.

The armada was turned around. The men were miserable cooped up on the ships. Many were seasick from the pitching seas. Private Felix Branham said, "We wanted to go. This sounds crazy, but we'd been sitting in England so long, we wanted to go and get this thing over with and go home."

Soldiers valued small packets of comfort items, including razor blades, cigarette papers, matches, chocolate, a brush, and even eyeglasses.

The airborne troops were much less affected since they were not in the cramped quarters of a ship, but they, too, were miserable. As the rain began, it turned airfields into mud, and the winds blew tents away. The delay was a huge letdown. Paratrooper Edward Boccafogli of the 82nd Airborne said, "It seemed to take everything right out of your stomach. A couple of tents collapsed and one was hit by lightning. The fellows were trapped underneath the canvas."

In the afternoon of June 4, Staggs again reviewed the weather charts. He thought he detected that one of the fronts in the Atlantic had slowed down. If that were the case, there might be a short period of better weather before the next storm front arrived. Many on his staff thought that the weather would not improve, but Staggs was convinced that it would. That evening he went to Southwick House to brief General Eisenhower as planned.

The Supreme Command consisted of (left to right) Lieutenant General Omar Bradley, U.S. Forces Commander; Admiral Sir Bertram Ramsay, Allied Sea Commander; Britain's Air Chief Sir Arthur Tedder, Deputy Supreme Commander; General Dwight D. Eisenhower, Supreme Commander; General Sir Bernard Montgomery, Commander of Allied Land Forces; Air Chief Marshal Sir Trafford Leigh-Mallory, Air Commander in Chief; and Lieutenant General Walter Bedell Smith, U.S. Army, Chief of Staff.

When he arrived at 9:30, it was pouring rain, and the wind was driving it sideways into the glass panes. Eisenhower and his staff looked gloomy. Staggs began his report by saying that the weather on June 6 would not be ideal. In fact, it would be barely tolerable. But the good news was that the winds should die, and the rains should end for a little while. The generals cheered when they heard the forecast, and Eisenhower ordered that the fleet be given the signal to sail again for Normandy. There would be one final meeting at 4 a.m. on June 5. That would be the last chance to recall the armada if the weather had not improved.

At 3:30 General Eisenhower awoke in his command trailer. The rain was driving down as hard as ever, and the wind was shaking the windows in Southwick House. When Staggs addressed the assembled generals, he announced that he was even more

Gliders carried many airborne troops into battle. The British *Horsa* was slightly larger than the American *Waco.* They were towed by C-47s and Halifax bombers, then released over their target areas.

This planeload, or "stick," of British paratroopers is on its way to Normandy. When it's time, each man will "stand up and hook up" his static line to a cable that runs down the center of the plane. These lines will pull open the parachutes as the men jump from the plane.

certain that the weather would improve, but only for a little while. The bad news was that it would deteriorate again in 36 hours.

General Eisenhower asked all of his generals for their thoughts. Again opinion differed. He made the final decision. "Okay, let's go." The assault would be made the following morning, June 6, 1944.

Across the Channel, German weatherman Walter Stoebe looked at the same charts that Staggs had examined and concluded that the weather would not improve. He advised that an Allied invasion on June 6 would be impossible. With that information, Field Marshal Rommel left Normandy to go to Germany for his wife's birthday.

The invasion began on the wings of the airborne. In particular, on the wings of six British bombers towing six British gliders, each with a crew of 30 men. They would be the tip of the spear of the great June 6th attack.

Gliders had the advantage of putting all their men on the ground together, in one spot, instead of scattered as would happen with a parachute jump. The disadvantage of gliders was that if one of these plywood craft crashed, all 30 of its men would be lost.

This red beret was worn by a paratrooper in the British Army.

The six gliders held 180 soldiers under the command of Major John Howard, who had been given a daring mission to capture two bridges in Normandy. These bridges were over the Orne River and the Caen Canal. The two waterways were 400 yards apart and ran parallel to each other from the French city of Caen to the English Channel.

If Major Howard and his men could seize the bridges intact, the Allies could use them to connect the invasion beaches to the British paratroopers who would drop after the gliders. It would also give General Eisenhower a way to break out of the invasion area after his forces landed, since his bombers were destroying all the other bridges to prevent the Germans from coming in.

Major Howard's force was called Company D, Ox and Bucks. Ox and Bucks was short for Oxfordshire and Buckinghamshire Regiment. Howard, who had been briefed about the mission six weeks before, suspected that the Germans had wired the bridges with explosives and that they were set to blow up if any attempt was made to capture them. This meant that Howard's force would have only a few minutes to capture the bridges before the Germans detonated the explosives.

Major John Howard (above) commanded British Company D, Oxfordshire and Buckinghamshire Regiment, known as Ox and Bucks. They were the first troops to land in Normandy on D-Day. Gliders #1, #2, and #3 (left) landed near the bridge over the Caen Canal.

If Howard and his men captured the bridge on the Caen Canal intact, they would transmit the word "Ham." If they captured the bridge on the Orne River, they would transmit "Jam." If by some miracle they could capture them both intact, they would transmit "Ham and Jam!"

Major Howard trained his six platoons so that each one knew the others' jobs. In early June they were quarantined in restricted areas, waiting for the order to go. Each day a messenger on a motorbike arrived from headquarters to give Howard a single-word order. No word meant anything to him except one: "Cromwell."

That one word meant that he would attack that very night. On June 4 the rider came as usual and whispered "Cromwell." Howard prepared his men, but the fierce storm forced a cancellation of the order. The next day, even though the weather seemed just as bad, the rider again came and gave Howard the same code word.

"We were up by our gliders by ten o'clock," said Major Howard, "and I took my seat opposite the open door. We shut the doors, and right on the dot at 2256 [10:56 p.m.], we were airborne, towed into the sky by our Halifax bomber."

The other five gliders took off right behind: #2 had David Wood's platoon; #3, Sandy Smith's; #4, Tony Hooper's, along with Brian Priday, Howard's second-in-command; #5, Dennis Fox's; and #6, Tod Sweeney's.

The flight across the Channel took just over an hour. As the small force crossed the coast of France, they cast themselves free from their bombers and began their glide toward the area of the bridges. After a ten-mile glide, Jim Wallwork, the pilot in

#1 glider, suddenly saw the parallel silver strips of the Orne River and the Caen Canal glowing in the moonlight. He headed straight for the Caen Canal and saw the land rushing up toward him. His glider hit the ground at about 95 miles per hour. Wallwork deployed the tail parachute to slow the glider down, and it came to rest with its nose just through the barbed wire in the field only 50 yards from the bridge. The impact of landing had ripped off the nose wheel and collapsed the cockpit. Wallwork and his co-pilot were thrown through the front windshield, but they survived.

John Howard struggled out of the wrecked glider. His watch had stopped at 16 minutes past midnight. He and his men were the first soldiers to land on French soil for D-Day. Howard told his lieutenant, Den Brotheridge, "Get your chaps moving!" In less than two minutes, the men of the Ox and Bucks captured the other side of the bridge. Unfortunately Lieutenant Brotheridge was killed in the attack.

Gliders #2 and #3 landed just a minute apart, firmly securing the bridge in Allied hands. Gliders #5 and #6 landed at the other bridge on the Orne River and seized it.

Corporal Fred Tappenden, the radio operator, lay on the road and began transmitting, "Ham and Jam; Ham and Jam." But no one answered him. "Hello Four Dog, hello Four Dog, Ham and Jam; Ham and Jam," Tappenden repeated over and over. In his frustration he finally transmitted, "Hello Four Dog, Ham and Jam; Ham and Jam, Ham and bloody Jam; why don't you answer me?" What he didn't know was that the person he was trying to contact had lost his radio. Howard's force had succeeded, but his men could not transmit to tell anyone. Their elation at capturing the bridges was dampened by the news that Glider #4 was missing. This meant that one-sixth of the entire force, along with Howard's second-in-command, Captain Brian Priday, was presumed lost.

But Captain Priday, Lieutenant Hooper, and the other men of glider #4 were in a fight of their own. Their tow plane had dropped them off course, and in trying to find the bridges, the pilot had made a very soft landing by a silvery stream of water. What he thought was the Orne River bridge was really a bridge on the Dives River, ten miles away. After a brief fight, British troopers quickly captured the bridge. As day broke they discovered their error and began to work their way toward John Howard. Escaping and evading the German forces, they finally arrived at their commander's

Members of the Screaming Eagles 101st Airborne Division camouflage their faces in preparation for their jump into France. Many gave each other Mohawk haircuts.

location in the early hours of the following morning. A very surprised John Howard was delighted to see them.

While John Howard and his men were boarding their gliders for the assault on the bridges of the Orne River and the Caen Canal, thousands of American paratroopers with blackened faces, Mohawk haircuts, razor-sharp knives, and overloaded packs struggled to climb on board aircraft and gliders that would take them across the English Channel to Normandy. These men were the paratroopers of the 101st and 82nd Airborne Divisions—the Screaming Eagles and the All Americans. Thirteen thousand of these troopers would jump into France.

General Eisenhower visited some of the men of the 101st Division during the hours before they took off. He walked through the ranks, telling the men not to worry, that they had the best equipment and leaders. One of the men piped up and said, "We ain't worried, General. It's the enemy that ought to worry now."

The 101st Airborne were in the first wave of airplanes. Their objective was the French town of Carentan. The 82nd would be in the second wave, 15 miles behind. Their objective was the town of Sainte-Mère-Église. These towns controlled the roads leading to Utah Beach. The paratroopers were to seize and hold these roads so that the German Army could not move to attack the American soldiers who would be landing on that beach.

When the troopers went to their aircraft, they were surprised to see that black and white stripes had been painted on the wings and fuselage of each airplane. This had been done in the 24 hours prior to takeoff to identify them to Allied forces as friendly

General Eisenhower visited many airborne troops before their takeoff. Here he speaks to men from the 101st Airborne Division at the airfield at Greenham Commons in England. Giving a thumbs-up sign, Ike tells a soldier from Kansas to "go get 'em."

aircraft. Ground forces had orders to shoot down any planes that did not have stripes.

As the long daylight hours of June 5 turned into darkness around 10 p.m., the last troopers were aboard, and the planes started their engines and taxied out onto the runways. More than 800 aircraft, flying in a formation nine planes wide and 300 miles long, took off and formed a giant sky train that carried the airborne troopers to Normandy. It took great flying skills to avoid midair collisions, since radio silence had to be maintained. The tiny blue dot on each plane's tail was all a pilot could see of the aircraft in front of him.

General Eisenhower watched the planes take off from Greenham Commons. As the last one disappeared into the night, he turned to his driver and said simply, "Well it's on." He had prepared and equipped his soldiers as best he could. Now he could only watch and wait. He was confident that these young men, many of them just teenagers, could accomplish their difficult mission. Others on his staff were opposed to the mission. His air marshal, Leigh-Mallory, thought it would be a bloodbath. Intelligence showed that a fresh German division had moved into the drop area, and the whole countryside bristled with German antiaircraft guns. Leigh-Mallory thought that 80 percent of the paratroopers could be killed, wounded, or captured.

Earlier Eisenhower had scribbled a note taking responsibility should the invasion fail: "Our landings…have failed. And I have withdrawn the troops. My decision to attack at this time and place was based on the best information available. The troops, the air and the Navy did all that bravery and devotion to duty could do. If any blame attaches to the attempt it is mine alone." It was June 5, but Ike had so many things on his mind that he dated the note "July 5."

It took the Screaming Eagles just over an hour to fly from England to Normandy. "The men were quiet," said Sergeant Carwood Lipton. "Each with his own thoughts." But as they passed over the coast of Normandy, the Germans began shooting at the planes with antiaircraft guns.

Sergeant Dan Furlong said, "You could see the shells coming up. They looked like Roman candles. And when they hit, it would sound just like someone threw a keg of nails against the side of the plane."

Many of the planes swerved to avoid the intense fire, and some of the pilots increased speed to try to escape the streams of green and yellow that reached into the sky. To many of the troopers, these colorful streams of steel were hypnotizing. They were deadly but beautiful, just like fireworks on the Fourth of July.

Finally the red light came on in the C-47 airplanes, and the stick commanders gave the order to "stand up and hook up." Paratrooper boots stomped on the steel decks of the planes, and there was the metallic sound of snap fasteners clicking shut as each man's static line was attached to a cable that ran down the center of the plane. Trooper Carl Cartledge said, "The green light popped on and, Geronimo, we all jumped. I've never been so glad to get out of an airplane in my life. The parachute slammed open; the planes were gone, taking the tracers with them."

The air over France was filled with Screaming Eagles. It was also filled with falling debris—burning aircraft, detached rifles, helmets, and packs ripped from the troopers

Streaks of light from antiaircraft fire, like that shown below, lit up the sky as planes carrying paratroopers approached their drop zones. Many troopers described the fire as the biggest Fourth of July fireworks they ever saw.

Darkness veiled the jump into Normandy so there are no photographs of the actual scene. This image shows planes discharging their men in a cloud of mushrooming parachutes over a drop zone in another part of Europe.

by the impact of the parachutes' opening shock. It was mass confusion, as the troopers landed in trees, hedgerows, and farm fields and on barns. Few landed in their designated zones. In ones and twos, they tried to find their way and make contact with their units. Some did; most did not. Some joined other units and fought with them until they could find their own squads and platoons. Others attacked Germans wherever they could find them.

The scattered drop had an unexpected benefit. Enemy commanders concluded that the American force was bigger than it was, so they did not aggressively attack.

Meanwhile, the 82nd Airborne Division was heading toward its target: Sainte-Mère-Église. The town was important because whoever controlled it controlled the roads leading to the port of Cherbourg and to Utah Beach.

The drop zones for the All Americans were to the northwest of the site. After landing, the paratroopers would move toward the town and seize it. One plane released its troopers directly over the town instead of over the fields on the outskirts. This was very dangerous because light from a burning building directly across from the church was illuminating the sky. The townspeople, watched closely by German soldiers, were passing buckets of water from the water pump next to the church to the burning building.

Suddenly, many little white shapes appeared in the night sky over the town square. What looked like "little mushrooms" to the people below were the parachutes of the descending troopers. The German soldiers immediately began firing up at the Americans.

One of the troopers was 17-year-old Private Ken Russell, who had joined the Army when he was only 15 by telling the recruiters he was older. That very night, his high school class back in Tennessee was having its graduation and prom. His friends were home celebrating in tuxedos, with pretty girls to take to the dance, while he was jumping into combat in France.

As he descended, he could see the whole scene below him: the burning building, the townspeople passing buckets of water, the Germans firing up, the gigantic church looming up from the square. "Lieutenant Cadish, H.T. Bryant, and Laddie Tlapa landed on telephone poles down the street," said the young paratrooper. "It was like they were crucified there. We were all sitting ducks coming down. The heat drew the

Shoulder patches of the 101st Airborne Division's Screaming Eagles (top) and the 82nd Airborne's All Americans

Private Ken Russell (above) hung from the belfry of the church at Sainte-Mère-Église. Another All American, Private John Steele, dangled from the site now marked by the effigy of a paratrooper (right). Steele was captured, but Russell freed himself and single-handedly knocked out an antiaircraft site nearby.

nylon chutes toward the fire, and the air to feed the fire was actually drawing us into it."

Russell watched in horror as one of the paratroopers sailed into the flames. "I heard him scream one time before he was engulfed, and he didn't scream any more." Another of his fellow troopers, John Blanchard, landed in the trees across from the church. Hanging dead in the same trees was trooper Blankenship, who had been shot on the way down. Blanchard struggled to release himself from his parachute by cutting frantically at the cord risers until he finally sawed his way through and fell to the ground. In his panic to free himself, Blanchard had cut off part of his finger but didn't realize it until the next day.

Russell spiraled toward the ground. As the Germans started shooting, people ran from the square. He was relieved to see that he was not being drawn into the fire, but his relief was short-lived. He was heading directly toward the massive belfry of the church.

"I finally hit the roof of the church," he said, "and a couple of my lines snagged on the gargoyles on the belfry, and I was suspended with my boots just hanging off the roof." He was 20 feet off the ground. Looking up, he saw a strange sight. Close to the top of the belfry another trooper was hanging lifelessly almost 50 feet above the ground. It was trooper John Steele. (Steele was actually playing possum so the Germans would think he was dead and not shoot him.)

Russell tried to reach the knife strapped to his boot so he could cut himself free. He knew that he would fall 20 feet, but he also knew that if he stayed where he was, German soldiers would kill him. As hard as he tried, however, he could not grab his knife. Then Russell's worst fears came true. A German soldier coming around from the other side of the church aimed his weapon, first at Steele and then at Russell. But before the soldier could shoot, he was distracted by a third paratrooper.

Sergeant John Ray, who had jumped last from the plane, crashed to the ground next to the church. "Sergeant Ray had missed the roof," said Russell. "He landed next to the church, and when he did, the German soldier shot him in the stomach. But before he died, he got his pistol out and when the soldier turned around to shoot Steele and me, Ray shot him first. He saved our lives before he died."

Russell finally freed himself, dropped to the ground, and ran into the countryside. He was alone, but he was a trained warrior. He relied on his training and distinguished himself in combat. He single-handedly destroyed an antiaircraft position that was firing at the planes overhead and was awarded the Bronze Star for heroism. He was part of a handful of paratroopers who desperately held on to Sainte-Mère-Église. Of the 16 men who jumped from the plane with him, only 6 survived. John Steele was dragged into the belfry when the Germans found him alive. He was taken prisoner but was rescued several days later by advancing Americans. As the night came to an end, the Screaming Eagles and the All Americans had succeeded in seizing the roads that led to Utah Beach. They had blocked the route that the German Army would need to counterattack the invasion forces that would be landing at daylight.

Sergeant John Ray, shown here with his dog, died from a stomach wound but not before he saved the lives of both Steele and Russell. Like all other American soldiers killed or wounded in action, he was awarded the Purple Heart medal (top).

Barrage balloons can be seen floating above ships that are part of the great Allied armada lined up in the English Channel off Normandy. Cables attached to the balloons act as anti-aircraft devices by shearing off the wings of low-flying enemy aircraft.

CHAPTER 5

the invasion

At 2 a.m. on June 6, the ships of the armada halted about 12 miles off the Normandy coast and began loading their soldiers into landing craft. The gigantic fleet had crossed the English Channel undetected by the enemy. The bad weather had kept German patrol boats and aircraft from venturing out. By 3 a.m. the small boats were circling, waiting for all the boats to fill before making their run to the beaches.

In preparation for the landing, more than 2,000 Allied aircraft conducted pre-dawn bombing raids on enemy positions along the beaches. German Private Franz Gockel's position was *Widerstansnest* 62, which means "resistance nest" number 62. It was a concrete-and-steel structure with openings for firing guns. There were 15 of these "pillboxes" along the area the Allies called Omaha Beach. "Debris and clouds of smoke enveloped us," he said. "The earth shook; eyes and nose were filled with dirt, and sand ground between our teeth. There was no hope for help."

Then came the Allied naval gunfire. "The wall of explosions approached, crackling, screaming, whistling, and sizzling, destroying everything in its path. I prayed for survival," said Gockel.

Despite the fearsome noise and shaking of the earth, the bombardment suddenly stopped. The German defenders all along the invasion area got up and dusted themselves off and were surprised that there were few casualties. The massive bombing and ship fire had failed to neutralize the German defensive positions.

Jacket of an American pilot decorated with hand-painted bombs to mark the number of missions flown

"There were six of us in my position," Gockel said, "and still none of us were injured." But his relief was short-lived. As the German defenders turned their eyes to the sea, they could not believe what they saw. "An endless fleet lay before our sector," the young private said. "Heavy warships cruised along as if passing in review. It was a spectacular but terrifying experience."

As Second Lieutenant Hans Heinz stared out from his position along the Normandy coast, a strange sight unfolded before him. Suddenly the low-hanging fog

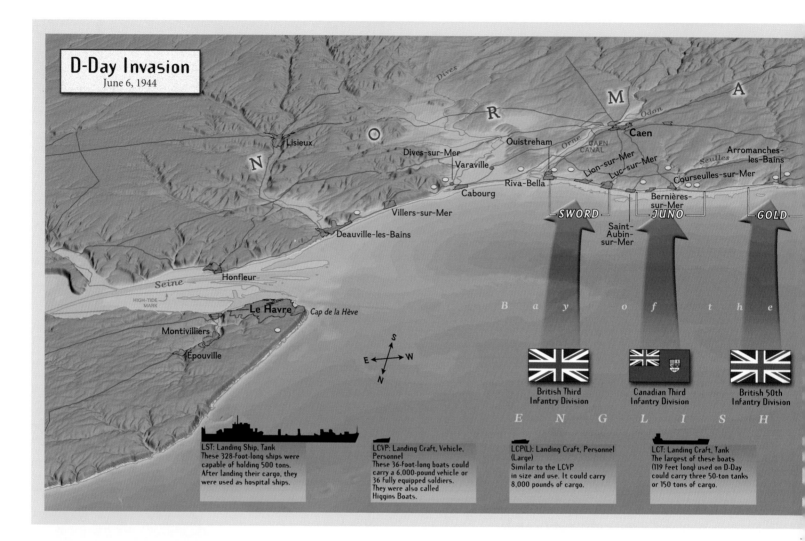

D-Day Invasion
June 6, 1944

LST: Landing Ship, Tank
These 328-foot-long ships were capable of holding 500 tons. After landing their cargo, they were used as hospital ships.

LCVP: Landing Craft, Vehicle, Personnel
These 36-foot-long boats could carry a 6,000-pound vehicle or 36 fully equipped soldiers. They were also called Higgins Boats.

LCP(L): Landing Craft, Personnel (Large)
Similar to the LCVP in size and use. It could carry 8,000 pounds of cargo.

LCT: Landing Craft, Tank
The largest of these boats (119 feet long) used on D-Day could carry three 50-ton tanks or 150 tons of cargo.

British Third Infantry Division

Canadian Third Infantry Division

British 50th Infantry Division

This map shows the five landing beaches along the coast of Normandy, where nearly 200,000 American, British, and Canadian forces transported by 5,300 ships, boats, and amphibious landing craft participated in the largest invasion by sea in the history of the world.

seemed to be pierced by the masts of many ships. It was as if sticks were protruding out of the clouds hugging the water. And then more of the ships came into view until the whole fleet lay exposed before him. "It was as though the entire world was confronting us," he said. "It was obvious to me that we could only contain this attack for one or two days."

The invasion began at 6:30 a.m. Due to the way the tides come ashore along the Normandy coast, the attacks on the various beaches could not be launched at the same time. First to land were the Americans at Utah and Omaha. Next were the British at Gold, then the Canadians at Juno, and finally the British came ashore at Sword at 7:30.

The boats carrying the American soldiers to Utah landed off their planned target area, but they landed intact, completely surprising the Germans. Twenty-eight of the 32 tanks in the first wave made it ashore and helped clear the beach of the weak resistance.

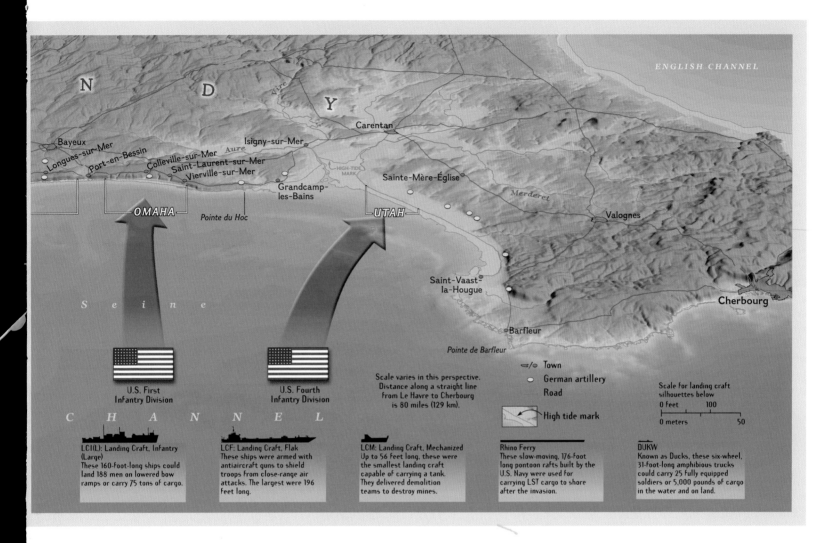

N D Y

Carentan

Bayeux
Longues-sur-Mer
Port-en-Bessin
Colleville-sur-Mer
Saint-Laurent-sur-Mer
Vierville-sur-Mer
Isigny-sur-Mer
Aure
HIGH-TIDE MARK
Sainte-Mère-Église
Merderet
Valognes

Grandcamp-les-Bains

OMAHA
Pointe du Hoc
UTAH

Saint-Vaast-la-Hougue

Cherbourg

S e i n e

Barfleur

Pointe de Barfleur

U.S. First
Infantry Division

U.S. Fourth
Infantry Division

Scale varies in this perspective.
Distance along a straight line
from Le Havre to Cherbourg
is 80 miles (129 km).

C H A N N E L

⊲/○ Town
○ German artillery
Road

High tide mark

Scale for landing craft
silhouettes below
0 feet   100
0 meters   50

LCI(L): Landing Craft, Infantry (Large)
These 160-foot-long ships could land 188 men on lowered bow ramps or carry 75 tons of cargo.

LCF: Landing Craft, Flak
These ships were armed with antiaircraft guns to shield troops from close-range air attacks. The largest were 196 feet long.

LCM: Landing Craft, Mechanized
Up to 56 feet long, these were the smallest landing craft capable of carrying a tank. They delivered demolition teams to destroy mines.

Rhino Ferry
These slow-moving, 176-foot long pontoon rafts built by the U.S. Navy were used for carrying LST cargo to shore after the invasion.

DUKW
Known as Ducks, these six-wheel, 31-foot-long amphibious trucks could carry 25 fully equipped soldiers or 5,000 pounds of cargo in the water and on land.

The soldiers, undeterred by their landing error, attacked and moved off the beach. By two o'clock the soldiers had linked up with members of the airborne divisions that had sealed off the approaches to the beach from the Germans. The landings at Utah succeeded beyond the wildest expectations of the Allied planners, thanks to the airborne operation.

One of the most difficult challenges the Allies faced was gaining control of heavily defended Pointe du Hoc. This hundred-foot-high piece of land jutted into the Bay of the Seine between Utah and Omaha Beaches. The Germans had fortified the land at the top with big guns that were able to fire on both beaches. General Eisenhower knew that this fortification could be a lot of trouble for the landing soldiers, so he ordered a group of Rangers to scale the steep, rugged cliffs and destroy the guns.

The Rangers fired ropes attached to hooks called grapnels to the top of the cliffs,

The tip of Pointe du Hoc juts into the English Channel between Utah and Omaha Beaches. Silencing the German guns atop this strategic position was one of the most important objectives of the Allies on D-Day.

Sergeant Lomell commanded Company D, Second Ranger Battalion at Pointe du Hoc on D-Day.

where they snagged barbed wire on the ground. Having gained a firm hold, the Rangers were able to pull themselves up, hand over hand. Once at the top, they attacked the German defenders and rushed to the fortifications holding the guns.

But the concrete emplacements had no guns. The Germans had replaced them with telephone poles to fool Allied planes taking aerial photographs. The Rangers secured the position and moved inland a little ways to block the road that ran all along the Normandy coast.

Two sergeants, Len Lomell, commander of the group, and Jack Kuhn, noticed a dirt path, with hedges on either side, leading between two farm fields. They followed the road, looking for the guns. They hadn't gone far when Sergeant Lomell, looking over the hedges, whispered, "There they are!" Five big guns were sitting in a small field. They were aimed at Utah Beach. The gun crews were at the far end of the field, talking.

Kuhn stood guard while Lomell squeezed through the hedge. Once on the other side, Lomell activated two thermite (heat-producing) grenades and placed them into the gears of two of the guns. The grenades burned silently with white-hot heat and melted the gears designed to swing the gun and raise the barrel. Soon the mechanisms were destroyed, leaving the guns useless. Since there were five guns and Lomell had only two grenades, he and Kuhn ran back to the men on the road to get more. When they returned to the field, the Germans were still at the far end. Lomell squeezed through the hedge and destroyed the gears of the three other guns. Then, wrapping his jacket around his rifle stock, he quietly smashed the gun sights. Thanks to the two sergeants, those German guns were not able to fire on Omaha or Utah Beach on D-Day.

Also achieving great success were the British landings at Gold Beach and Sword Beach. The British Third Division and 50th Division made great progress and moved aggressively inland from those beaches. By two o'clock, elements of the British amphibious forces from Sword had linked up with Major John Howard's glider forces at the bridges on the Orne River and the Caen Canal. The forces at Gold achieved most of their objectives, driving the German forces in front of them.

At Sword Beach, a young student nurse named Jacqueline Noel had gone down to the beach around nine o'clock the morning of June 6 to retrieve a bathing suit she had left after a previous day's swim. But she got caught up in the invasion traffic, and the British soldiers would not let her go back for security purposes. "When I saw the invasion fleet," she said, "it was something you just can't imagine. It was boats, boats, boats, and boats at the end, boats at the back, and planes coming over. If I had been a German, I would have looked at this, put my arms down, and said, 'That's it. Finished!'"

But the German soldiers who saw the fleet were not throwing down their arms. At the Canadian beach called Juno and at the American beach called Omaha, things were not going well at all.

Several miles to the west of Gold Beach and just a few miles east of Pointe du Hoc, the Americans landed at Omaha Beach. Unlike the other beaches in the invasion area, a long cliff loomed one hundred feet above the sand, dominating the landing area. It was here in February 1944 that the German commander Rommel had seen the beach as a possible invasion site and ordered it strengthened. For the next four months, the German forces had created concrete and steel defensive positions like the one manned by Private Gockel.

British troops and equipment come ashore at Sword Beach after the main landing at 0730 hours. They soon moved off the beach and headed inland to meet up with airborne troops.

Members of the U.S. First Infantry Division look anxiously over the sides of their landing craft as it approaches Omaha Beach. The smoke on the hillside above the beach is from a fire caused by Allied naval gunfire.

Soldiers struggle ashore amidst enemy obstacles and destroyed vehicles and landing craft. The Americans were pinned down on Omaha until late morning when some managed to scramble to the high ground behind the beach.

The Allied planners had taken aerial photographs of the German defenses and had assigned the United States air forces to drop 13,000 bombs to neutralize these strongpoints just minutes before the beach landings. But the sky was very overcast, and the pilots had to bomb by instrument instead of by seeing the target. Because of the danger of dropping bombs on approaching American landing craft hidden by the clouds, General Eisenhower had approved a plan that would delay the bomb release by several seconds. As a result, most of the bombs sailed over Omaha and the German fortifications, landing as much as three miles inland.

At Widerstansnest 62, Private Gockel watched the first wave of boats plow through the surf and touch down on the sand. The American soldiers jumped from the craft to the beach and started running between the obstacles. Gockel had lain flat in his position during the massive Allied bombardments. Now he and the rest of the defenders manned their weapons.

"The first closely packed troops sprang from their boats," he said. "Some were in knee-deep water, others up to their chests. There was a race across the beach toward the low stone wall, which offered the only protection. Now we sprang into action. Now we heard the first machine-gun bursts, and within seconds, the first assault wave troops collapsed after making only a few steps."

The German fire all along the beach was tremendous, especially on the right flank near Widerstansnests 72 and 73. Twenty minutes after the first wave landed, there were few American soldiers who were not dead or wounded. The second and third waves did no better. They were virtually annihilated by the strong German defenses.

"On came the second wave," Gockel said, "and again the race across the beach, and again the defensive fires. More and more of American comrades were killed."

Robert Sales, a radio operator in the second wave, described the approach to the beach. "The ramp went down, and Captain Zappacosta was the first man off, and they just riddled him. Everybody who went off, they just cut them down."

The young radio operator stumbled off the side of the ramp into the water and felt himself dragged to the bottom by the weight of his radio. When he came back up, he was out in front of the boat, almost on the beach. He looked back at his boat and watched as the rest of the men scrambled to jump off the ramp into the water. But as

German Private Franz Gockel defended the position at Omaha Beach known as Widerstansnest 62.

51

fast as the men came out of the boat, the bullets from the machine guns hit them.

"We were cut to pieces," said Sales, the sole survivor of the 30 men in his boat.

Soldiers tried to get off the deadly beach. In twos and fours and other small bands, they struggled to make it through the barbed wire and mines toward the cliffs. It seemed the fire there was less intense. As the soldiers crawled forward, a group of half-tracks (small vehicles with wheels in the front and tracks like a tank in the back) landed. Each had an automatic weapon mounted on it. Surprisingly, they were not fired on by the German guns. A soldier who was pinned down on the beach began frantically pointing to a bunker that was dominating that section of the beach. It was Widerstansnest 65.

Sergeant Hyman Haas, a section leader in charge of two of the half-tracks, immediately went into action. "I directed the vehicles back into the water and we took up firing positions about twenty-five feet apart," he said. "My first three shots were low, but the next ten shots went into the porthole of the pillbox. That was the end of that. Whatever was in there was destroyed."

With the concrete position destroyed, American soldiers were able to advance. Haas and his men had opened up the first lane to exit off the beach. The German line was finally broken. Over the next two hours, other small units led by men like Sergeant Haas also broke the defensive line in front of their positions. With the help of naval gunfire, the Americans slowly pushed the German soldiers out of their positions. By eleven o'clock, the soldiers were able to get off the beach and make their way up the cliff into the fields. But the effort to take the beach had been tremendously costly in lives and equipment. There were well over 2,000 casualties. The beach was strewn with wrecked vehicles and burning ships and boats. Some infantry units had lost most of their soldiers. The fight on that beach forever earned it the name "Bloody Omaha."

Meanwhile the Canadian Third Division was involved in its own inferno at a section of beach code-named Juno. It was supposed to land at 7:30 a.m., but tricky currents and the tide forced the boats off course, putting it behind schedule by 30 minutes. By the time the Canadian force approached the beach, the rising tide had covered many of the obstacles the Germans had anchored in the sand. The coxswains

Private Robert Sales came ashore at Omaha in the second wave. Of the 30 men in his boat team, he was the sole survivor.

American wounded at Omaha Beach await evacuation. Many of the men were caught in deadly crossfire on the beach. Others were injured while disembarking in deep water or when German fire sank their landing craft.

Canadian soldiers of the Third Division come ashore at Juno Beach. Their main casualties occurred when offshore mines blew up their boats.

navigating the boats struggled to avoid colliding with them, but this was difficult because the waves were coming in at an angle. As the boats hit the obstacles, their bottoms were ripped out. Those that collided with mines were blown up. Sergeant Stanley Dudka of the North Nova Scotia Highlanders said, "Going in there were obstacles and the beaches had not been cleared. No one had landed where we did."

Wilfred Bennett from the Royal Winnipeg Rifles described his section of the beach. "We hit the water waist deep, and men were falling in the water. And then they fell on the beach. The machine gun fire was devastating." Whole boat teams were lost in the surf of Juno Beach. One after another, many boats were destroyed. Some just sank, while others blew up in fiery explosions. The men and equipment in these doomed craft sank to the bottom.

Some of the soldiers finally landed and were able to overcome the German fire, but the mines continued to take a heavy toll out in the surf. As the morning wore on, half of the boats were damaged and almost one-third of the landing craft were lost. By late morning, the Canadian division gained control of the beach, but it had suffered the loss of more than one thousand men.

As D-Day ended, the Allies were far short of the objectives set up in the planning of the day. But all along the five-beach invasion front soldiers were dug in. They had kept the German Army from hurling them back into the sea. The Navy was now able to bring ships in to unload directly on the beaches. The attack had been a total surprise. Field Marshal Rommel's decision to leave Normandy to go home for his wife's birthday was a critical mistake. In the early hours of the invasion, he was not present to command the German defensive forces.

There would be many more months of hard fighting, but at least the first day was over. Radios in the free world broadcast that the invasion had succeeded in landing and that despite some difficulties, things were going according to plan. In Paris, Henry Goldsmith, a member of the French Resistance, made it his business to go to a German restaurant on the night of June 6. He spoke perfect German, so he blended with the crowd. Soldiers there bragged that the Allies had suffered terrible casualties and predicted that within 24 hours the Allies would be defeated. How wrong they were.

Eleven months after D-Day, Germany surrendered.

Canadian soldier Sergeant Stanley Dudka of the North Nova Scotia Highlanders

A Mulberry Harbor is in operation at Arromanches-les-Bains after the invasion. Vehicles drive from the deepwater unloading area across a floating causeway to the beach. A storm on June 19 severely damaged this harbor and destroyed the one established at Omaha Beach.

NEW ORLEANS STATES | EXTRA

VOL. 66—NO. 107   New Orleans, La., Monday, May 7, 1945   PRICE CITY AND COUNTRY 5c

GERMANY SURRENDERS

Reims, France, May 7.—Germany surrendered unconditionally to the Western Allies and Russia at 2:41 a. m., French Time today.

(This was at 8:41 p. m., Eastern War Time Sunday.)

The surrender took place at a little red schoolhouse which is headquarters of General Eisenhower.

The surrender which brought the war in Europe to a formal end after five years, eight months and six days of bloodshed and destruction was signed for Germany by Colonel General Gustav-Jodl.

Jodl is the new chief of staff of the German army.

It was signed for the supreme Allied command by Lieutenant General Walter Bedell Smith, chief of staff for General Eisenhower.

It was also signed by General Ivan Susloparoff for Russia and by General Francois Sevez for France.

AMERICAN TANKS DRIVE THROUGH THE TRAIL OF RUINS THAT ONCE WAS GERMANY

THE "BIG THREE" AT TEHERAN IN 1944 AS THEY PLANNED TODAY'S VICTORY

Headline from a New Orleans newspaper announces Germany's surrender and with it the long-awaited end of the war in Europe on May 7, 1945. War in the Pacific continued until September 2, when Japan signed the surrender documents.

56

D-Day was the beginning of the end of Nazi Germany. Until the Allies actually broke through the Atlantic Wall and landed on the continent of Europe, there was no way that they could decisively defeat the German *Wehrmacht,* or War Machine. The early battles fought in North Africa, Sicily, and Italy resulted in important victories, but they were not decisive enough to end the war. They were simply stepping stones to a final showdown that would engage the German Army on its homeland.

Although the Allies liberated Rome on June 4, 1944, Germany still maintained its ability to wage war. It could still manufacture the tools of war and mobilize its population to fight.

The Soviet Army, although successfully fighting the Germans on the Eastern Front, was a long way away from entering the German heartland. If the Germans had defeated the Normandy invasion, they could have concentrated their forces on defeating the Soviets.

The Soviet Union was a reluctant ally at best. There was nothing to stop Joseph Stalin from making a separate agreement with Germany if the Allies did not open a second front. After all, that's what had happened in World War I. Nor were the Soviets blameless in the start of Hitler's war. In exchange for signing a pact promising not to interfere with Hitler's aggression, the Soviet Union was given half of Poland by the Nazi dictator.

Either by defeating the Soviets or by signing an agreement with them, Hitler would have eliminated all threats to his power and could have continued to spread his tyranny over Europe. His persecutions of people he considered undesirable, especially the Jews, would have gone unchallenged. His concentration camps that worked people to death as slave labor would have continued. His death camps that murdered people by the millions and burned their bodies simply because he considered them undesirable would have multiplied, expanding the Nazis' grisly work. A new Dark Age would have dawned, robbing people of their freedom. The Nazi elite would have exercised the power of life and death over all the people they ruled.

Only an attack that would lead to a final, victorious invasion of the German homeland could bring an end to this monstrous dictatorship. The invasion of Normandy on D-Day was that attack. Eleven months later Hitler's Third Reich ceased to exist.

WORLD WAR II TIME LINE

This time line shows some of the key events of the two major areas, or theaters, of war: Europe (blue columns) and the Pacific (tan columns). Operations in Africa are commonly considered as part of the European theater. The Pacific theater included action on islands in the Pacific Ocean as well as on the mainland of Asia. A separate time line for D-Day appears in the yellow columns.

By the time war was declared in Europe, Adolf Hitler had already annexed the Rhineland, Austria, and part of Czechoslovakia. Meanwhile Japan was expanding its empire in Asia and the Pacific. By the time the Japanese attacked Pearl Harbor, they had occupied much of China and the eastern part of mainland Southeast Asia.

WAR IN EUROPE

1939

AUGUST
The Soviet Union and Germany sign a nonaggression pact known as the Molotov-Ribbentrop Agreement in which the Soviets agree not to interfere with Hitler's plans to invade Poland.

SEPTEMBER
Hitler invades Poland as the German Army unleashes *blitzkrieg,* or "lightning warfare." France and Great Britain declare war on Germany.

Soviet Union grabs land in eastern Poland under the terms of its pact with Germany.

OCTOBER
Polish resistance ceases to exist after the Germans capture 700,000 Poles and the Soviets take 200,000. Nazis begin persecuting Polish Jews.

NOVEMBER
Soviet Union invades Finland.

DECEMBER
Soviet Union is expelled from the League of Nations for attacking Finland.

1940

MARCH
Finland and the Soviet Union sign a peace treaty. The Finns retain their independence but lose territory.

APRIL
The German Army invades Denmark and Norway.

MAY
Germany invades Belgium, the Netherlands, Luxembourg, and France. The evacuation of the British Army from France at Dunkirk begins. The Netherlands, Belgium, and Luxembourg fall to Hitler.

British Prime Minister Neville Chamberlain resigns; Winston Churchill becomes the new prime minister.

JUNE
Italy under dictator Benito Mussolini enters the war as Germany's ally.

France surrenders. General Charles de Gaulle is recognized as the leader of the Free French movement.

JULY
Churchill rejects a peace pact proposed by Hitler. The Battle of Britain begins with bombing raids over the English Channel.

AUGUST
Soviet Union annexes Estonia, Latvia, and Lithuania and announces neutrality in hostilities with Germany and Britain.

German air forces (Luftwaffe) attack southern England.

SEPTEMBER
The London Blitz begins as Germany launches a series of bombings that continues for 57 nights and claims the lives of more than 40,000 Londoners. Air raids over England continue until spring 1945.

OCTOBER
Hitler postpones Operation Sealion (the invasion of Britain).

Italy invades Greece. Greek Army throws Italians onto the defensive.

Franklin Roosevelt is elected to his third term as U.S. President.

DECEMBER
Hitler plans to invade the Soviet Union.

1941

FEBRUARY
Germany and Spain sign a secret defensive pact.

MARCH
Franklin Roosevelt promises aid to countries fighting Germany until victory is achieved.

Yugoslavia signs a pact with Hitler.

APRIL
Germany invades and takes control of Greece and Yugoslavia.

MAY
The German battleship *Bismarck* engages and sinks the British battle cruiser *Hood.* One week later the British Navy sinks the *Bismarck.*

JUNE
Ignoring a nonaggression pact, Germany invades the Soviet Union in Operation Barbarossa.

SEPTEMBER
The German Army occupies Kiev and lays siege to Leningrad (now St. Petersburg) in the Soviet Union.

OCTOBER
Germans attack Moscow. Soviet dictator Joseph Stalin announces that "Moscow will be defended to the last." To date, the Soviet Union has lost 600,000 square miles of territory to the Germans.

German submarine sinks the destroyer *Reuben James.* It is the first U.S. ship sunk in the European war. Roosevelt, wearing a black armband, says the event will not affect German-American relations.

DECEMBER
Soviets launch a counteroffensive to stop the German advance on Moscow.

Hitler declares war on the U.S.

1942

JANUARY
Nazis plan to exterminate the Jews.

MAY
German Army starts a third counteroffensive in North Africa.

JUNE
German Afrika Korps captures the Libyan city of Tobruk.

AUGUST
German Army begins the Battle of Stalingrad (now Volgograd).

NOVEMBER
British Army's defeat of Afrika Korps at El Alamein is a turning point in the war in North Africa.

Soviet forces break the siege of Stalingrad and counterattack, putting the Germans on the defensive.

WAR IN THE PACIFIC

1940

JULY
Japan begins its advance into French Indochina on the mainland of Southeast Asia. In response, the U.S. stops exports of scrap iron and steel to Japan.

SEPTEMBER
Japan signs a pact allying it with Italy and Germany. The three countries are the chief members of the Axis powers.

1941

NOVEMBER
Talks between the U.S. and Japan break down. Japanese fleet secretly sets sail for Pearl Harbor.

DECEMBER
Japan attacks the U.S. naval base at Pearl Harbor and then Allied bases in the Philippines, Guam, Wake Island, Hong Kong, Malaya, and Singapore.

The U.S. declares war on Japan.

British surrender in Hong Kong. Japanese sink the two largest British warships, the *Repulse* and the *Prince of Wales,* near Singapore.

The Japanese defeat American forces on Guam and Wake Island.

Japanese troops launch large-scale invasion of the Philippines.

1942

FEBRUARY
Japan gains control of Singapore.

APRIL
U.S. and Filipino troops defending the Philippines' Bataan Peninsula are defeated. Many survivors die on their way to prison camps in what became known as the Bataan Death March.

Sixteen U.S. bombers, commanded by Lieutenant Colonel James Doolittle, launch a surprise air raid on Tokyo.

MAY
Japan gains control of the Philippines after the Battle of Corregidor.

In the Battle of the Coral Sea planes from U.S. aircraft carriers battle planes from Japanese carriers. The U.S. loses the *Lexington* but stops the Japanese advance on Port Moresby on the island of New Guinea.

JUNE
Outnumbered U.S. Navy crushes Japan's Navy in the Battle of Midway.

Japanese troops land on Alaska's Aleutian Islands.

AUGUST
U.S. Marines land on Guadalcanal and nearby islands. The fight to stop the Japanese from building an airfield there was the first in a long series of battles known as the Battle for the Solomon Islands.

OCTOBER
In the Battle of Santa Cruz the U.S. Navy loses the aircraft carrier *Hornet* but stops Japan's resupply of Guadalcanal.

DECEMBER
Tests by scientists in America prove it's possible to make an atomic bomb.

1943

FEBRUARY
German Sixth Army surrenders at Stalingrad. This halts Hitler's advance eastward and marks a turning point in the war in Europe.

APRIL
Lieutenant General Frederick Morgan is ordered to begin planning for a "full-scale assault against the Continent in 1944, as early as possible." The date of the assault would be known as D-Day.

MAY
Axis forces surrender in North Africa, giving Allied armies control of bases from which to launch an invasion of southern Europe.

JULY
Soviet Army, advancing westward, defeats German Army at Kursk in the war's biggest tank battle.

Allies invade Sicily off the tip of Italy.

Italian dictator Mussolini is removed from power. Italy secretly begins peace talks with the Allies.

SEPTEMBER
Italy surrenders to the Allies, but Germany continues to fight for control of Italy.

British and American troops land at Salerno and begin to push their way up the Italian peninsula.

NOVEMBER
Allied forces reach Cassino, just south of Rome, and meet heavy resistance from the German Army.

Roosevelt, Churchill, and Stalin meet in Tehran, Iran. At Stalin's insistence, priority is given to Operation Overlord, code name for the assault on Hitler's Atlantic Wall.

DECEMBER
D-Day, as the date of the invasion is known, is set for May 1, 1944.

JANUARY
The fighting on Guadalcanal ends with the evacuation of Japanese troops.

APRIL
Over Bougainville in the Solomon Islands U.S. air forces shoot down a plane carrying Admiral Yamamoto, the Japanese naval chief who planned the attack on Pearl Harbor.

NOVEMBER
U.S. Marines take Tarawa in the Gilbert Islands and learn lessons that improve future amphibious landings.

1944

JANUARY
Americans land at Anzio, in Italy.

Siege of Leningrad ends. Soviet Army pushes German Army back to Poland.

APRIL
U.S. planes begin bombing Berlin, Germany's capital.

JUNE
Allied forces liberate Rome. Severe weather forces D-Day to be postponed to June 6.

American, British, and Canadian forces land at Normandy on D-Day.

First German V-1 rocket bombs hit Great Britain.

AUGUST
Allies liberate Paris.

SEPTEMBER
Allies launch Operation Market-Garden into the Netherlands. The operation fails to break into Germany.

OCTOBER
First German V-2 rockets, flying close to the speed of sound, hit London.

Roosevelt is elected to a fourth term.

DECEMBER
Battle of the Bulge begins as the German Army attacks the Americans in the Ardennes Forest in Belgium.

FEBRUARY
General MacArthur begins his drive through the Pacific that will end with the recapture of the Philippines.

JUNE
U.S. Navy crushes final Japanese naval attack in the Battle of the Philippine Sea. The Japanese lost over 300 planes, giving the battle the name Great Marianas Turkey Shoot.

Powerful B-29 American bombers strike Japan, unleashing an air war that will last until summer 1945.

JULY
The capture of Saipan puts Tokyo within range of U.S. B-29 bombers.

U.S. Marines land on Guam and Tinian.

SEPTEMBER
U.S. carrier planes bomb the Philippines. Marines land at Peleliu.

OCTOBER
General MacArthur returns to the Philippines as the U.S. fleet defeats the Japanese fleet at Leyte Gulf in the largest naval battle in history. The Japanese unleash kamikaze pilots (the "divine wind") to fly their planes, with bombs, into U.S. ships.

D-Day / June 6, 1944

EVENTS LEADING UP TO D-DAY

(Times are given in military time: 0001 to 2400 hours.)

JANUARY
Dwight D. Eisenhower assumes duties as Supreme Commander, Allied Expeditionary Forces and changes D-Day from May 1 to June 5.

FEBRUARY
The plan for Operation Overlord, code name for the Allied invasion of Europe, is confirmed.

JUNE 3
Lead ships of the great armada move out into the English Channel and sail for France.

JUNE 4
The wings and fuselages of all Allied planes are painted with black and white stripes to distinguish them from enemy aircraft.

0400 Group Captain J. M. Staggs predicts bad weather for June 5. Eisenhower postpones D-Day for 24 hours until June 6. Ships are called back.

2130 Staggs predicts a break in bad weather for the morning of June 6.

2145 Eisenhower once again orders the armada to sail for France.

JUNE 5
0400 At the final meeting of the Allied Command at Southwick House Eisenhower says, "Okay, let's go." The invasion is on for June 6.

2256 Gliders of the British Sixth Airborne take off for France.

JUNE 6 D-DAY

0016
Glider forces of Major John Howard's Ox and Bucks seize bridges over the Orne River and Caen Canal. British paratroopers of the Sixth Airborne jump onto the Ranville Plain, in France.

0100–0300
Americans of the 82nd and 101st Airborne Divisions jump into France with orders to secure the towns of Sainte-Mère-Église and Carentan.

0520
Allied bombers hit enemy targets on the five invasion beaches.

0535
German shore batteries fire on the Allied armada in the English Channel.

0550
Allied naval bombardment begins and lasts for 30 minutes.

0630
Americans in the first assault waves land at Omaha and Utah Beaches.

0700–0730
U.S. Rangers assault Pointe du Hoc and Pointe et Raz de la Percée.

0730
British land on Gold and Sword Beaches.

0755
Canadians land on Juno Beach.

0830
Heavy German resistance forces landings at Omaha Beach to stop.

1309
Americans overcome resistance and move off Omaha Beach.

2400
Allied Army is successfully lodged in Normandy.

U.S. soldiers dig in along a seawall at Utah Beach.

1945

JANUARY
Nazi death camp at Auschwitz, in Poland, where almost two million Jews were killed, is liberated by the Allies.

Americans defeat the Germans in the Battle of the Bulge.

Soviet troops take control of Poland and march toward Berlin.

FEBRUARY
Churchill, Roosevelt, and Stalin meet in the Soviet city of Yalta to discuss the division of Germany and other postwar issues.

MARCH
U.S. soldiers cross the Rhine River into Germany at Remagen.

U.S. air forces conduct unrelenting bombing attacks against Germany.

APRIL
President Franklin Roosevelt dies in Warm Springs, Georgia.

Former Italian dictator Benito Mussolini is captured and executed by Italian partisans.

U.S. and Soviet forces meet at the Elbe River on the advance to Berlin.

More Nazi death camps are liberated by advancing Allied armies.

Adolf Hitler commits suicide in a Berlin bunker.

MAY
Germany surrenders on May 7 at Eisenhower's headquarters in France.

JANUARY
U.S. B-29s begin a series of massive firebomb attacks that will cause tremendous damage to Tokyo and other Japanese cities.

FEBRUARY
U.S. Marines land at Iwo Jima.

MARCH
The most damaging firebomb attack on Tokyo destroys much of the city and wipes out key industrial targets.

APRIL
U.S. Marines and Army land on Okinawa. Japan unleashes maximum kamikaze attacks.

AUGUST
A U.S. B-29 flying from Tinian Island drops an atomic bomb on Hiroshima on August 6. Three days later Nagasaki is the target of a second atomic bomb. Soviet Union declares war on Japan.

Japan's Emperor Hirohito accepts terms of surrender (August 14).

SEPTEMBER 2
Japan signs the surrender documents on the U.S.S. *Missouri* in Tokyo Bay.

bibliography

Every soldier on D-Day wore a set of dog tags like these for identification.

Ambrose, Stephen E. *D-Day June 6, 1944: The Climactic Battle of World War II*. New York: Simon & Schuster, 1994.

Ambrose, Stephen E. *Pegasus Bridge: June 6, 1944*. New York: Simon & Schuster, 1985.

Brown, Anthony Cave. *Bodyguard of Lies*. New York: Harper & Row, 1975.

Crookenden, Napier. *Dropzone Normandy*. New York: Charles Scribner's Sons, 1976.

D'Este, Carlo. *Decision in Normandy*. London: Collins, 1983.

Drez, Ronald J., ed. *Voices of D-Day: The Story of the Allied Invasion Told by Those Who Were There*. Baton Rouge, La: Louisiana State University Press, 1994.

Drez, Ronald J. *Twenty-Five Yards of War: The Extraordinary Courage of Ordinary Men in World War II*. New York: Hyperion, 2001.

Eisenhower, Dwight D. *Crusade in Europe*. Garden City, N.Y.: Doubleday, 1948.

Ewing, Joseph H. *The 29th: A Short History of a Fighting Division*. Paducah, Ky.: Turner Publishing, 1992.

Harrison, Gordon A. *Cross-Channel Attack*. Washington, D.C.: Office of the Chief of Military History. Department of the Army, 1951.

Historical Section European Theater of Operations Staff, eds. *Utah Beach to Cherbourg*. Nashville, Tenn.: Battery Press, 1984.

Lewin, Ronald. *Ultra Goes to War*. London: Hutchinson, 1978.

Mitcham, Samuel. *Rommel's Last Battle: The Desert Fox and the Normandy Campaign*. New York: Stein & Day, 1983.

Morrison, Samuel Eliot. *The Invasion of France and Germany, 1944-45*. (Volume 11 of *History of United States Naval Operations in World War II*.) Boston: Little, Brown, 1959.

U.S. Army Historical Section Staff, *Omaha Beachhead: June 6-June 13, 1944*. Nashville, Tenn.: Battery Press, 1984.

Weigley, Russell. *Eisenhower's Lieutenants: The Campaigns of France and Germany, 1944-45*. Bloomington: Indiana University Press, 1981.

A note about the quotes in this book:

Unless otherwise indicated, all quotes are taken from oral histories or memoirs archived in the National D-Day Museum in New Orleans, Louisiana.

Hitler's quote in Chapter 2 is taken from Samuel Mitcham, *Rommel's Last Battle: The Desert Fox and the Normandy Campaign* (New York: Stein & Day, 1983). Churchill's quote in Chapter 3 is taken from the tape archive, D-Day Museum, Portsmouth, England, and Anthony Cave Brown, *Bodyguard of Lies* (New York: Harper & Row, 1975). Eisenhower's quotes in Chapter 4 are from his book *Crusade in Europe* and from Stephen Ambrose's book *D-Day June 6, 1944: The Climactic Battle of World War II*. Eisenhower's quote on the back cover is from his written message to the troops just prior to D-Day.

index